D0464299

CARLA BARDI
RACHAEL LANE

Chocolate

50 DELICIOUS RECIPES

nextquisite

Copyright 2017 by Nextquisite Ltd, London

Project Director Anne McRae
Art Director Marco Nardi

Photography Brent Parker Jones
Text Nextquisite Archive
Editing Christine Price, Anne McRae
Food Styling Lee Blaylock
Layouts Aurora Granata

ISBN 978-1-910122-43-3

Printed in China

NOTE TO OUR READERS
Eating eggs or egg whites that are not completely cooked poses the possibility of salmonella food poisoning. The risk is greater for pregnant women, the elderly, the very young, and persons with impaired immune systems. If you are concerned about salmonella, you can use reconstituted powdered egg whites or pasteurized eggs.

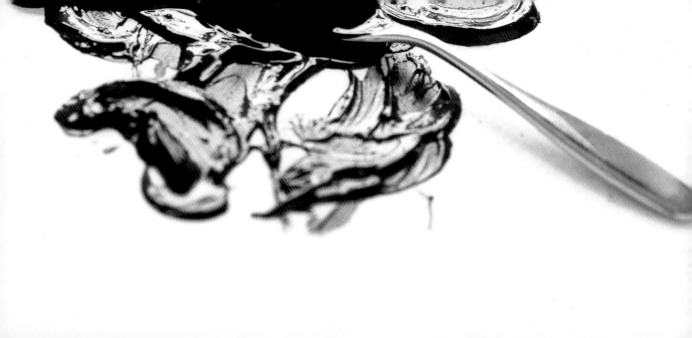

- 3 cups (450 g) all-purpose (plain) flour
- 1½ teaspoons baking soda (bicarbonate of soda)
- ½ teaspoon salt
- 1¼ cups (310 g) unsalted butter, softened
- 1½ cups (300 g) firmly packed light brown sugar
- 1 cup (200 g) sugar
- 1½ teaspoons vanilla extract (essence)
- 3 large eggs
- 1 pound (500 g) dark chocolate chips

Sift the flour, baking soda, and salt into a large bowl.

Beat the butter, both sugars, and vanilla in a large bowl with an electric mixer on medium-high speed until creamy. Add the eggs one at a time, beating until just combined after each addition.

With the mixer on low speed, gradually beat in the flour mixture. Stir in the chocolate chips by hand. Cover the bowl and chill for 1 hour.

Preheat the oven to 350°F (180°C/gas 4). Line three or four large baking sheets with parchment paper.

Scoop up heaped tablespoons of dough and roll into balls. Place on the prepared baking sheets, spacing about 3 inches (7 cm) apart.

Bake for 15–20 minutes, until the cookies are golden brown at the edges but still very soft in the center. Rotate the sheets halfway through for even baking.

Let the cookies cool on the baking sheets for 2–3 minutes, until they are firm enough to move. Transfer to a wire rack and let cool completely.

Makes 45–50
Preparation 20 min
+1 hr to chill
Cooking 15–20 min
Level 1

This recipe is based on the classic Toll House cookies that were first made in Massachusetts during the 1930s. You can vary them by replacing the dark chocolate chips with milk or white chocolate chips.

chocolate chip cookies

- 1⅔ cups (250 g) all-purpose (plain) flour
- 1½ teaspoons baking powder
- ¼ teaspoon salt
- ½ cup (120 g) unsalted butter, softened
- ¼ cup (60 ml) sunflower or peanut oil
- ¾ cup (150 g) firmly packed light brown sugar
- 1 large egg, lightly beaten
- ½ teaspoon vanilla extract (essence)
- 1 cup (180 g) white chocolate chips
- 1 cup (100 g) chopped walnuts

Sift the flour, baking powder, and salt into a medium bowl.

Beat the butter, oil, and brown sugar in a large bowl with an electric mixer on high speed until creamy.

Add the egg and vanilla, beating until just blended. With the mixer on low speed, gradually beat in the flour mixture, chocolate chips, and walnuts.

Form the dough into a 7-inch (18-cm) long log, wrap in plastic wrap (cling film), and refrigerate for at least 30 minutes.

Preheat the oven to 375°F (190°C/gas 5). Butter two large baking sheets.

Slice the dough ¼ inch (5 mm) thick and place 2 inches (5 cm) apart on the prepared baking sheets.

Bake for 10–12 minutes, until just golden at the edges. Rotate the sheets halfway through for even baking.

Let the cookies cool on the baking sheets for 2–3 minutes, until they are firm enough to move. Transfer to a wire rack and let cool completely.

Makes 28–30
Preparation 20 min
+ 30 min to chill
Cooking 10–12 min
Level 1

We have added a cup of chopped walnuts to these cookies, but you could replace them with almonds or macadamia nuts, if preferred.

white chocolate chip cookies

Cookies

- 1¼ cups (180 g) all-purpose (plain) flour
- ¼ cup (30 g) unsweetened cocoa powder
- ½ teaspoon baking powder
- ⅛ teaspoon salt
- ¾ cup (180 g) unsalted butter, softened
- ½ cup (100 g) firmly packed light brown sugar
- 2 cups (60 g) cornflakes
- 30 walnut halves, to decorate

Chocolate Frosting

- 2 cups (300 g) confectioner's (icing) sugar
- 3 tablespoons unsweetened cocoa powder
- ½ teaspoon vanilla extract (essence)
- 1–2 tablespoons boiling water

Cookies: Preheat the oven to 350°F (180°C/gas 4). Grease two large baking sheets and line with parchment paper.

Sift the flour, cocoa, baking powder, and salt into a bowl.

Beat the butter and brown sugar in a large bowl with an electric mixer on medium speed until creamy. With the mixer on low speed, gradually beat in the flour mixture until just combined. Stir in the cornflakes by hand.

Shape the dough into 30 even balls and place about ¾ inch (2 cm) apart on the prepared baking sheets. Flatten slightly with your hand.

Bake for 10–15 minutes, until firm to the touch. Rotate the baking sheets halfway through for even baking.

Let the cookies cool on the baking sheets for 2–3 minutes, until they are firm enough to move. Transfer to a wire rack and let cool completely.

Chocolate Frosting: Sift the confectioners' sugar and cocoa into a small bowl. Stir in the vanilla and enough boiling water to make a smooth frosting.

Spoon a dollop of the frosting onto each cookie and decorate with a walnut half. Allow the frosting to set before serving.

Makes 30
Preparation 15 min
Cooking 10–15 min
Level 1

Afghan cookies have relatively little sugar in the base which is made with plenty of butter and cornflakes. The sweetness is given by the delicious chocolate frosting.

afghan
cookies

- ¾ cup (180 g) salted butter, softened
- ¾ cup (150 g) sugar
- 2 teaspoons vanilla extract (essence)
- 1 large egg
- 2 cups (300 g) all-purpose (plain) flour
- ¼ cup (30 g) unsweetened cocoa powder

Beat the butter and sugar in a large bowl until pale and creamy. Beat in the vanilla and egg.

Gradually beat in the flour. Divide the dough into two equal portions. Beat the cocoa into one of the portions.

Shape both portions into oblongs. Wrap in plastic wrap (cling film) and chill for 30 minutes.

Roll both pieces of the dough into ¼-inch (5-mm) thick rectangles. Put the chocolate dough on top of the pale dough. Trim the edges to neaten. Roll up lengthwise like a jelly roll.

Wrap in plastic wrap and chill for 30 minutes.

Preheat the oven to 350°F (180°C/gas 4). Butter two large baking sheets or line with parchment paper.

Slice the dough into disks as thinly as you can. Place on the baking sheets, spacing well.

Bake for 12–15 minutes, until golden brown. Rotate the sheets halfway through for even baking.

Let the cookies cool on the baking sheets for 2–3 minutes, until they are firm enough to move. Transfer to a wire rack and let cool completely.

Makes 30–35
Preparation 20 min
+ 1 hr to chill
Cooking 12–15 min
Level 2

Change the flavor of the cookies
by replacing the vanilla extract
with 1 teaspoon of lemon extract
or ½ teaspoon almond extract.

pinwheel cookies

Cookies

- 1²/₃ cups (250 g) all-purpose (plain) flour
- 1 teaspoon baking powder
- ⅛ teaspoon salt
- ²/₃ cup (150 g) unsalted butter, softened
- ½ cup (100 g) sugar
- 1 large egg yolk
- 1 vanilla pod
- 1 cup (100 g) broken-up, dried, unsweetened banana chips

Glaze

- 7 ounces (200 g) dark chocolate, coarsely chopped

Cookies: Sift the flour, baking powder, and salt into a medium bowl.

Beat the butter and sugar in a large bowl with an electric mixer on high speed until creamy. Add the egg yolk, beating until just blended.

Scoop out the pulp from the vanilla pod and add to the mixture. Mix in the dry ingredients and banana chips to form a smooth dough.

Divide the dough in half. Form into 10-inch (25-cm) logs, wrap in plastic wrap (cling film), and chill for 30 minutes.

Preheat the oven to 350°F (180°C/gas 4). Line three large baking sheets with parchment paper.

Slice the dough ½ inch (1 cm) thick. Press the centers inward and taper the ends to form crescents. Place 1 inch (2.5 cm) apart on the prepared baking sheets.

Bake for 10–12 minutes, until just golden. Rotate the sheets halfway through for even baking.

Let the cookies cool on the baking sheets until they harden a little, 2–3 minutes. Transfer to racks and let cool completely.

Glaze: Melt the chocolate in a double boiler over barely simmering water, or in the microwave.

Dip one end of each cookie into the chocolate. Let stand on parchment paper for 30 minutes to set.

Makes 40
Preparation 30 min
+ 1 hr to chill & set
Cooking 10–12 min
Level 2

This recipe makes a lot of cookies. Prepare them for a party or special occasion when you are expecting a lot of guests.

chocolate
banana kipferl

Cookies

- 1⅓ cups (350 g) salted butter, softened
- ½ cup (75 g) confectioners' (icing) sugar
- ½ teaspoon vanilla extract (essence)
- 2 cups (300 g) all-purpose (plain) flour
- ⅓ cup (50 g) cornstarch (cornflour)
- ¼ cup (30 g) unsweetened cocoa powder

Filling

- 1 cup (250 g) mascarpone cheese
- 1 tablespoon confectioners' (icing) sugar
- 2 ounces (60 g) dark chocolate
- ½ teaspoon vanilla extract (essence)

Cookies: Preheat the oven to 350°F (180°C/gas 4). Line two large baking sheets with parchment paper.

Beat the butter and confectioners' sugar in a large bowl with an electric mixer on medium speed until pale and creamy. Add the vanilla and mix well.

With the mixer on low speed, gradually beat in the flour and cornstarch. Divide the mixture evenly between two bowls and add the cocoa to one bowl. Mix well, adding a little water if the mixture is too stiff.

Spoon the mixtures into piping bags fitted with star nozzles. Pipe out 16 walnut-size cookies from each mixture, spacing them 1 inch (2.5 cm) apart on the prepared baking sheets.

Bake for 15–20 minutes, until firm to the touch. Rotate the sheets halfway through for even baking.

Let the cookies harden on the baking sheets for 2–3 minutes. Transfer to racks and let cool completely.

Filling: Mix the mascarpone and sugar in a bowl until smooth, then divide between two bowls.

Melt the chocolate in a double boiler over barely simmering water, or in the microwave. Add the chocolate to one bowl of filling and the vanilla to the other, stirring both until smooth.

Sandwich the vanilla cookies together with the chocolate mascarpone filling and the chocolate cookies with the vanilla mascarpone filling.

Makes 16
Preparation 30 min
Cooking 15-20 min
Level 1

These indulgent cookies have
a divine melt-in-your-mouth
texture that goes beautifully with
a cup of tea or coffee.

melting
moments

Macarons

1 cup (150 g) confectioners' (icing) sugar
1 tablespoon unsweetened cocoa powder
1 cup (100 g) ground almonds
2 large egg whites

Filling

3 ounces (90 g) dark chocolate, coarsely chopped
1 tablespoon skimmed milk, warmed a little

Macarons: Line three large baking sheets with edible rice paper. Sift the confectioners' sugar and cocoa into a bowl. Stir in the almonds.

Beat the egg whites in a medium bowl with an electric mixer on medium speed until stiff and dry. Add half the almond and cocoa mixture to the meringue and use a large metal spoon to fold it in. Fold in the remaining almond and cocoa mixture.

Transfer to a pastry (piping) bag and pipe out 24–30 circles about 1½ inches (3–4 cm) in diameter on the baking sheets, spacing about 1 inch (2.5 cm) apart.

Put the baking sheets in a cool dry place and let rest for 30 minutes.

The macarons should harden slightly and will not stick to your finger if you poke them gently.

Preheat the oven to 350°F (180°C/gas 4). Bake for 15–20 minutes, until risen and smooth on top. If they begin to split, crack the oven door open a fraction to cool it down slightly.

Remove from the oven and let the macarons cool completely on the baking sheets.

Filling: Melt the chocolate in a double boiler over barely simmering water, or in the microwave. Stir in the warm milk until smooth. Leave to cool and thicken, about 15 minutes.

Sandwich the macarons together in pairs, and serve.

Makes 12–15
Preparation 30 min
+ 45 min to rest
Cooking 15–20 min
Level 3

Macarons are made with a mixture of egg whites, ground nuts (usually almonds), and sugar. Crisp and meringue-like in texture, they make a delicate dessert.

chocolate
macarons

- 10 small pears, peeled, stalks still attached
- 3 cups (750 ml) water
- 2 teaspoons vanilla bean paste
- 1½ cups (300 g) superfine (caster) sugar
- 2 tablespoons unsweetened cocoa powder + ¼ cup (30 g) extra
- 7 ounces (200 g) dark chocolate, finely chopped
- ¾ cup (180 g) salted butter
- 1⅓ cups (200 g) all-purpose (plain) flour
- 1 teaspoon baking powder
- 2 large eggs, lightly beaten

Preheat the oven to 350°F (180°C/gas 4). Butter ten muffin pans.

Use a melon baller to scoop out the base and core from each pear.

Combine the water, vanilla paste, and half the sugar in a medium saucepan over low heat. Cook and stir until the sugar dissolves, about 5 minutes.

Bring to a boil. Add the pears and simmer gently, turning occasionally, until the pears are tender, about 10 minutes. Use a slotted spoon to transfer the pears to a plate to drain.

Whisk the 2 tablespoons of cocoa into the syrup. Simmer until the syrup thickens slightly, 10–15 minutes. Set aside until ready to serve.

Combine the chocolate and butter in a double boiler over barely simmering water, stirring until smooth. Remove from the heat.

Add the flour, baking powder, eggs, extra cocoa, and remaining sugar to the chocolate mixture and stir until well combined.

Spoon the mixture into the prepared pans. Gently press a pear into the center of each cupcake.

Bake for 20 minutes, until a skewer comes out clean. Set aside for 15 minutes to cool.

Carefully remove from the pans and divide among serving plates. Drizzle with the chocolate syrup, and serve.

Makes 10
Preparation 45–50 min
+ 15 min to cool
Cooking 45–50 min
Level 2

These cupcakes make a striking
dessert. You will need small, tasty
pears, such as Corella.

chocolate
pear cupcakes

Cupcakes

- 3½ ounces (100 g) dark chocolate, coarsely chopped
- ⅓ cup (90 ml) light (single) cream
- ⅔ cup (100 g) all-purpose (plain) flour
- ½ cup (75 g) finely ground hazelnuts
- 2 tablespoons unsweetened cocoa powder, sifted
- 1 teaspoon baking powder
- ⅛ teaspoon salt
- ⅓ cup (90 g) unsalted butter, softened
- 1 cup (200 g) firmly packed light brown sugar
- 2 large eggs
- 1 tablespoon hazelnut liqueur
- ¼ cup (40 g) hazelnuts, coarsely chopped

Frosting

- 3½ ounces (100 g) dark chocolate, coarsely chopped
- ½ cup (120 g) chocolate hazelnut spread (Nutella)
- 2 tablespoons coarsely chopped hazelnuts, to decorate

Cupcakes: Preheat the oven to 325°F (170°C/gas 3). Line a standard 12-cup muffin pan with paper liners.

Melt the chocolate and cream in a double boiler over barely simmering water. Set aside to cool.

Combine the flour, ground hazelnuts, cocoa, baking powder, and salt in a small bowl.

Beat the butter and brown sugar in a medium bowl with an electric mixer on medium-high speed until creamy. Add the eggs one at a time, beating until just blended after each addition.

With the mixer on low speed, add the flour mixture and chocolate mixture. Stir in the liqueur and hazelnuts by hand.

Spoon the batter into the cups, filling each one three-quarters full.

Bake for 25–30 minutes, until risen and firm to the touch.

Transfer the muffin pan to a wire rack. Let cool completely before removing the cupcakes.

Frosting: Melt the chocolate in a double boiler over barely simmering water, or in the microwave. Remove from the heat and stir in the chocolate nut spread. Let cool a little.

Spoon the mixture into a pastry (piping) bag fitted with a star nozzle and pipe on top of each cupcake. Sprinkle with the coarsely chopped hazelnuts, and serve.

Makes 12
Preparation 30 min
Cooking 25–30 min
Level 2

Serve these cupcakes as dessert
or with a cup of tea or coffee
at anytime of the day. You can vary
the flavor by using ground almonds
and almond liqueur instead of
hazelnuts and hazelnut liqueur.

nutty chocolate
cupcakes

Cupcakes

- 3½ ounces (100 g) dark chocolate, coarsely chopped
- ⅓ cup (90 ml) light (single) cream
- 1 cup (150 g) all-purpose (plain) flour
- 2 tablespoons unsweetened cocoa powder
- 1 teaspoon baking powder
- ⅛ teaspoon salt
- ⅓ cup (90 g) unsalted butter, softened
- 1 cup (200 g) sugar
- 2 large eggs
- 2 tablespoons cherry brandy
- ¼ cup (120 g) drained maraschino cherries, coarsely chopped + 12 extra, to decorate

Topping

- ⅔ cup (150 ml) heavy (double) cream
- 2 tablespoons confectioners' (icing) sugar
- ½ tablespoon cherry brandy
- 2 ounces (60 g) dark chocolate, coarsely grated

Cupcakes: Preheat the oven to 350°F (180°C/gas 4). Line a standard 12-cup muffin pan with paper liners.

Melt the chocolate and cream in a double boiler over barely simmering water, stirring until smooth. Remove from the heat and let cool.

Sift the flour, cocoa, baking powder, and salt into a small bowl.

Beat the butter and sugar in a bowl with an electric mixer on medium speed until pale and creamy. Add the eggs one at a time, beating until just blended after each addition.

With the mixer on low speed, add the flour mixture, chocolate mixture, and cherry brandy.

Spoon the batter into the prepared cups, filling each one three-quarters full.

Bake for 20–25 minutes, until risen and firm to the touch.

Transfer the muffin pan to a wire rack. Let cool completely before removing the cupcakes.

Topping: Whip the cream in a small bowl until it begins to thicken. Gradually add the confectioners' sugar, whisking until soft peaks form. Stir in the cherry brandy.

Put a dollop of topping and a cherry on top of each cupcake. Top with grated chocolate, and serve.

Makes 12
Preparation 30 min
Cooking 20–25 min
Level 1

These cupcakes are inspired by the classic Black Forest Cake (see our recipe on page 58). They make a wonderful dessert.

black forest cupcakes

Cupcakes

- 1 ounce (30 g) dark chocolate, coarsely chopped
- 2 tablespoons light (single) cream
- 1 cup (150 g) all-purpose (plain) flour
- 1 teaspoon baking powder
- 1/8 teaspoon salt
- 1/3 cup (90 g) unsalted butter, softened
- 1 cup (200 g) sugar
- 1 teaspoon vanilla extract (essence)
- 2 large eggs
- 2 tablespoons milk
- 1 tablespoon unsweetened cocoa powder, sifted

Frosting

- 1/2 cup (120 g) unsalted butter, softened
- 1/2 teaspoon vanilla extract (essence)
- 1 1/2 cups (225 g) confectioners' (icing) sugar
- 1 tablespoon unsweetened cocoa powder

Cupcakes: Preheat the oven to 325°F (170°C/gas 3). Line a standard 12-cup muffin pan with paper liners.

Melt the chocolate and cream in a double boiler over barely simmering water. Set aside to cool.

Sift the flour, baking powder, and salt into a small bowl. Beat the butter, sugar, and vanilla in a bowl with an electric mixer on medium speed until pale and creamy. Add the eggs one at a time, beating until just blended after each addition.

With the mixer on low speed, add the flour mixture. Divide the mixture between two bowls. Stir the milk into one bowl and the chocolate mixture and cocoa into the other.

Spoon the batters alternately into the prepared cups, filling each one three-quarters full.

Bake for 25–30 minutes, until risen and firm to the touch.

Transfer the muffin pan to a wire rack. Let cool completely before removing the cupcakes.

Frosting: Beat the butter and vanilla in a small bowl until light and fluffy. Gradually add the confectioners' sugar, beating until well mixed.

Divide the frosting between two bowls. Add the cocoa to one. Place alternate spoonfuls of vanilla and chocolate frosting into a pastry (piping) bag fitted with a star nozzle. Pipe a swirl on top of each cupcake.

Makes 12
Preparation 30 min
+ time to cool
Cooking 25–30 min
Level 2

The creamy frosting on these cupcakes is superb. If preferred, you can make it all a chocolate flavor by doubling the amount of cocoa to 2 tablespoons.

chocolate swirl cupcakes

Slice

- 1 cup (250 ml) sweetened condensed milk
- ¼ cup (60 g) salted butter
- 1 teaspoon vanilla extract (essence)
- 3 tablespoons unsweetened cocoa powder
- 2 cups (250 g) coarsely crushed plain sweet cookies
- ½ cup (75 g) walnuts, coarsely chopped
- 3 tablespoons shredded (desiccated) coconut

Frosting

- 1½ cups (225 g) confectioners' (icing) sugar
- 2 tablespoons unsweetened cocoa powder
- 1 tablespoon boiling water
- 2 teaspoons salted butter

Slice: Line an 8-inch (20-cm) square cake pan with aluminum foil, leaving a 2-inch (5-cm) overhang on two sides.

Stir the condensed milk and butter in a small saucepan over low heat until the butter melts.

Remove from the heat and add the vanilla. Sift in the cocoa, stirring to combine.

Combine the crushed cookies, walnuts, and coconut in a medium bowl. Stir into the condensed milk mixture until well combined.

Spread in the prepared pan, smoothing the top with the back of a spoon. Cover and refrigerate until firm, 3–4 hours.

Frosting: Sift the confectioners' sugar and cocoa into a small bowl.

Stir the water and butter in a small bowl until the butter is melted. Gradually pour the water mixture into the frosting, stirring until smooth.

Spread over the slice and refrigerate for 15 minutes to set.

Remove from the refrigerator and lift out onto a chopping board using the overhanging foil.

Dip a sharp knife into boiling water. Cut the slice into bars or squares, and serve.

Makes 12–16
Preparation 15 min
+ 3–4 hr to set
Cooking 2–3 min
Level 1

This slice is perfect for a children's birthday party. It is very simple to make and children will also enjoy helping to prepare it.

no-bake
chocolate slice

- ⅔ cup (150 g) salted butter
- 1¼ cups (250 g) sugar
- 1 cup (150 g) unsweetened cocoa powder
- 2 teaspoons water
- 1 teaspoon vanilla extract (essence)
- 2 large eggs, chilled
- ⅓ cup (50 g) all-purpose (plain) flour
- 1 cup (120 g) walnut pieces
  Confectioners' (icing) sugar, to dust

Preheat the oven to 350°F (180°C/gas 4). Butter an 8-inch (20-cm) square baking pan. Line with parchment paper or aluminum foil, leaving a 2-inch (5-cm) overhang on two sides.

Melt the butter in a medium saucepan over medium-low heat. Simmer until the butter stops foaming, stirring often, about 5 minutes. Remove from the heat and add the sugar, cocoa, water, and vanilla. Stir to blend. Let cool for 5 minutes.

Add the eggs to the warm mixture one at a time, beating until just combined after each addition.

When the mixture looks thick and shiny, add the flour and stir until blended. Beat vigorously for 1 minute. Stir in the walnuts.

Spoon the batter into the prepared pan, smoothing the surface.

Bake for 20–25 minutes, until a toothpick inserted into the center comes out with just a few moist crumbs attached.

Leave the brownies in the pan for 5 minutes then lift carefully onto a board using the overhanging paper or foil.

Dust with the confectioners' sugar (or cocoa), cut into squares, and serve warm or at room temperature.

Makes 12-16
Preparation 15 min
Cooking 20-25 min
Level 1

Brownies should be almost crisp on top but still gooey in the center. The secret lies in the cooking time and oven temperature. Experiment with this classic recipe until you get it just right.

chocolate walnut brownies

Chocolate Batter

- 1 cup (150 g) all-purpose (plain) flour
- ¼ cup (30 g) unsweetened cocoa powder
- ½ teaspoon baking powder
- ½ teaspoon salt
- 8 ounces (250 g) dark chocolate, coarsely chopped
- ½ cup (120 g) unsalted butter
- 1¼ cups (250 g) sugar
- 3 large eggs

Cream Cheese Batter

- 4 ounces (120 g) cream cheese, softened
- 2 tablespoons unsalted butter, softened
- ¼ cup (50 g) sugar
- 1 large egg
- 2 tablespoons all-purpose (plain) flour

Preheat the oven to 350°F (180°C/gas 4). Grease a 9-inch (23-cm) square baking pan. Line with parchment paper or aluminum foil, leaving a 2-inch (5-cm) overhang on two sides.

Chocolate Batter: Sift the flour, cocoa, baking powder, and salt into a bowl.

Melt the chocolate and butter in a double boiler over barely simmering water.

Remove from the heat and beat in the sugar. Add the eggs one at a time, beating until just combined after each addition. Gradually add the flour mixture, mixing until just combined.

Cream Cheese Batter: Beat the cream cheese and butter in a bowl until smooth. Beat in the sugar, egg, and flour.

Place alternate spoonfuls of the chocolate and cream cheese batters in the prepared pan. Swirl with a knife to create a marbled pattern.

Bake for 30–40 minutes, until a toothpick inserted into the center comes out with just a few moist crumbs attached.

Leave in the pan for 1 hour. Lift the brownies carefully onto a board using the overhanging paper or foil. Transfer to a rack and let cool completely. Cut into squares, and serve.

Makes 16
Preparation 20 min
+ 1 hr to rest
Cooking 30–40 min
Level 1

For a change, stir a handful of
raspberries or blueberries into
the cream cheese mixture
before baking.

marbled brownies

Cake

- 8 ounces (250 g) dark chocolate, broken into chunks
- 1 cup (250 g) salted butter
- 1 cup (200 g) firmly packed light brown sugar
- 1/3 cup (90 ml) water
- 1/2 cup (120 ml) sour cream
- 2 large eggs, beaten
- 1 1/2 cups (225 g) all-purpose (plain) flour
- 1/3 cup (50 g) unsweetened cocoa powder

Colored sprinkles (hundreds and thousands, jimmies) to decorate

Frosting

- 3 1/2 ounces (100 g) dark chocolate, coarsely chopped
- 3/4 cup (180 ml) sweetened condensed milk
- 1/2 cup (120 g) salted butter

Cake: Preheat the oven to 325°F (170°C/gas 3). Line a 9-inch (23-cm) square baking pan with parchment paper.

Combine the chocolate, butter, brown sugar, and water in a saucepan and gently melt over low heat. Set aside for 2 minutes, then stir in the sour cream and eggs.

Stir in the flour and cocoa until well combined. Spoon the batter into the prepared pan.

Bake for 50–55 minutes, until a skewer inserted into the center comes out clean. Place the pan on a wire rack and let cool completely, about 1 hour.

Frosting: Combine the chocolate, sweetened condensed milk, and butter in a double boiler over barely simmering water, stirring until smooth. Remove from the heat.

Chill in the refrigerator until spreadable, about 15 minutes.

Remove the cooled cake from the pan and peel off the paper. Spread with the frosting and top with the colored sprinkles. Slice and serve.

This rich chocolate fudge cake is
simple to make. Serve with tea
or coffee or as a special dessert.

chocolate
fudge cake

Base

- 8 ounces (250 g) dark chocolate, coarsely chopped
- ¼ cup (60 g) unsalted butter
- ½ cup (100 g) sugar
- 2 large eggs
- ⅔ cup (100 g) all-purpose (plain) flour
- ⅓ cup (50 g) finely ground almonds
- ½ teaspoon baking powder
- ⅛ teaspoon salt
- ⅓ teaspoon almond extract (essence)

Cheesecake

- 1 pound (500 g) cream cheese, softened
- 1 cup (250 g) sweetened condensed milk
- ¼ cup (60 ml) sour cream
- 2 teaspoons vanilla extract (essence)

Frosting

- 4 ounces (120 g) dark chocolate, coarsely chopped
- 2 tablespoons unsalted butter

Base: Preheat the oven to 350°F (180°C/gas 4). Butter and flour an 8 x 12-inch (20 x 30-cm) baking pan. Line with parchment paper or aluminum foil, leaving a 2-inch (5-cm) overhang on the two long sides.

Melt the chocolate, butter, and sugar in a double boiler over barely simmering water.

Remove from the heat and beat in the eggs, flour, almonds, baking powder, salt, and almond extract.

Spoon the batter into the prepared pan, smoothing the top with the back of the spoon.

Bake for about 30 minutes, until a toothpick inserted into the center comes out clean. Place the pan on a wire rack and let cool completely.

Cheesecake: Beat the cream cheese, condensed milk, sour cream, and vanilla with an electric mixer on low speed until smooth and creamy. Spread over the cooled cake in the pan. Chill in the refrigerator until set, at least 2 hours.

Frosting: Melt the chocolate and butter in a double boiler over barely simmering water. Let cool a little then spread evenly over the cheesecake layer. Chill for at least 30 minutes.

Lift the cake carefully onto a board using the overhanging paper or foil. Cut into bars, and serve.

Makes 16
Preparation 30 min
+ 2½ hr to chill & set
Cooking 30 min
Level 2

These bars make a great dessert.
Keep in the refrigerator until ready
to slice and serve.

chocolate
cheesecake bars

Base

- ⅓ cup (50 g) all-purpose (plain) flour
- ½ teaspoon baking powder
- ¼ cup (30 g) unsweetened cocoa powder
- 3½ ounces (100 g) dark chocolate, chopped
- ¼ cup (60 g) salted butter
- 2 large eggs
- ¾ cup (150 g) sugar

Filling

- 8 ounces (250 g) white chocolate, chopped
- ½ cup (120 ml) double (heavy) cream
- 2 teaspoons peppermint extract (essence)
  Green food coloring

Frosting

- 5 ounces (150 g) dark chocolate
- 1 tablespoon light corn (golden) syrup
- ¼ cup (60 g) salted butter

Base: Preheat the oven to 350°F (180°C/gas 4). Grease a 9-inch (23-cm) square pan. Line with parchment paper or aluminum foil, leaving a 2-inch (5-cm) overhang on two sides.

Sift the flour, baking powder, and cocoa into a bowl.

Melt the chocolate and butter in a double boiler over barely simmering water. Let cool to room temperature.

Beat the eggs and sugar in a bowl with an electric mixer on medium-high speed until pale and thickened. Fold the chocolate mixture into the egg mixture. Fold in the flour mixture. Pour into the prepared pan.

Bake for 15–20 minutes, until the top is just set. Let cool completely in the pan on a wire rack.

Filling: Put the chocolate in a heatproof bowl. Bring the cream to a boil, then pour over the chocolate. Gently stir until smooth. Stir in the peppermint and food coloring.

Chill until thickened, about 15 minutes. Spread over the brownie, then chill for 45 minutes.

Frosting: Melt the chocolate, syrup, and butter in a double boiler over barely simmering water. Let cool a little, then spread over the filling. Chill for 1 hour.

Lift carefully onto a board using the overhanging paper or foil. Cut into bars and serve.

Makes **12**
Preparation **30 min**
+ 2 hr to chill
Cooking **15–20 min**
Level **2**

You could leave the green food coloring out of the filling, but it does add a touch of color to the finished dish. Serve on St. Patrick's Day!

chocolate mint bars

Base

- ¾ cup (180 g) unsalted butter
- ⅓ cup (70 g) sugar
- 1 vanilla pod, split and seeds scraped out
- 1½ cups (225 g) all-purpose (plain) flour

Caramel

- 1 cup (250 g) unsalted butter
- 1 (14-ounce/400-g) can sweetened condensed milk
- 4 tablespoons light corn (golden) syrup
- 1 teaspoon salt

Topping

- 12 ounces (350 g) milk chocolate

Base: Preheat the oven to 350°F (180°C/gas 4). Grease an 8-inch (20-cm) square baking pan. Line with parchment paper or aluminum foil, leaving a 2-inch (5-cm) overhang on two sides.

Rub the butter, sugar, vanilla seeds, and flour together in a bowl to make a coarse dough. Press the dough firmly into the prepared pan and prick all over with a fork.

Bake for 5 minutes, then reduce the oven temperature to 300°F (150°C/gas 2). Bake for 35 minutes. Let cool in the pan.

Caramel: Combine the butter, condensed milk, syrup, and salt in a saucepan and bring to a boil. Simmer over very low heat for 10 minutes.

Pour the caramel mixture over the base. Chill until the caramel has cooled and hardened slightly, about 30 minutes.

Topping: Melt the chocolate in a double boiler over barely simmering water, or in the microwave. Set aside to cool a little.

Pour the topping over the caramel. Chill until the chocolate has set, about 30 minutes.

Lift the cake carefully onto a board using the overhanging paper or foil. Cut into squares, and serve.

Makes 12–16
Preparation 30 min
+ 1 hr to chill & set
Cooking 45 min
Level 2

These delicious squares make a
superb dessert for special occasions.
If preferred, replace the milk chocolate
in the topping with dark chocolate.

chocolate
caramel
squares

Base

1 large egg
¼ cup (50 g) sugar
½ cup (120 g) salted butter, softened
1 teaspoon vanilla extract (essence)
3 tablespoons unsweetened cocoa powder
2 cups (250 g) graham cracker or digestive biscuit crumbs
1 cup (150 g) unsweetened shredded (desiccated) coconut
½ cup (60 g) finely chopped pecans

Creamy Filling

¼ cup (60 g) salted butter, softened
3 tablespoons heavy (double) cream
2 cups (300 g) confectioners' (icing) sugar
½ teaspoon vanilla extract (essence)

Frosting

5 ounces (150 g) dark chocolate, chopped
2 tablespoons salted butter

Base: Preheat the oven to 350°F (180°C/gas 4). Butter a 9 x 13-inch (23 x 33-cm) baking pan.

Beat the egg and sugar in a large bowl with an electric mixer on high speed until pale and thick. Use a wooden spoon to stir in the butter, vanilla, cocoa, graham cracker crumbs, coconut, and pecans.

Firmly press the mixture into the prepared pan to form a smooth, even layer.

Bake for 10–15 minutes, until firm to the touch. Let cool completely in the pan on a wire rack.

Creamy Filling: Beat the butter, cream, confectioners' sugar, and vanilla in a large bowl with an electric mixer on high speed until well blended.

Spread the mixture over the base and freeze for 15 minutes.

Frosting: Melt the chocolate and butter in a double boiler over barely simmering water, or in the microwave.

Spread over the creamy filling. Chill until set, about 1 hour. Cut into bars, and serve.

Makes 20
Preparation 40 min
+ 1¼ hr to chill
Cooking 10–15 min
Level 2

This recipe is based on the classic
treat from the city of Nanaimo, in
British Columbia.

nanaimo bars

Panforte

- 2 tablespoons raisins
- ½ cup (60 g) walnuts, chopped
- ¼ cup (30 g) almonds, chopped
- ¼ cup (30 g) hazelnuts, chopped
- ¼ cup (30 g) pine nuts
- ⅔ cup (150 g) mixed candied (glacé) peel, cut into small cubes
- ⅓ cup (50 g) unsweetened cocoa powder
- 4 ounces (120 g) dark chocolate, chopped
- ½ teaspoon each ground cinnamon, nutmeg, coriander, freshly ground black pepper
- ¼ cup (60 ml) honey, warmed
- 2⅓ cups (350 g) all-purpose (plain) flour
- ¼ teaspoon fennel seeds
- ½ cup (120 ml) warm water + extra, as needed

Glaze

- 8 ounces (250 g) dark chocolate, chopped

Panforte: Soak the raisins in a small bowl of warm water for 15 minutes. Drain well.

Preheat the oven to 325°F (170°C/gas 3). Butter and flour a 10-inch (25-cm) square cake pan.

Mix the walnuts, almonds, hazelnuts, pine nuts, candied peel, raisins, cocoa, chocolate, cinnamon, nutmeg, coriander, and pepper in a large bowl. Stir in the honey, flour, fennel seeds, and enough warm water to make a stiff dough.

Spoon the dough into the prepared pan, smoothing it evenly with the back of the spoon.

Bake for 25–30 minutes, until firm to the touch. Cool in the pan for 30 minutes. Turn out onto a rack and let cool completely.

Glaze: Melt the chocolate in a double boiler over barely simmering water. Set aside to cool for 10 minutes. Spread over the cake.

Let set for at least 1 hour. Cut into small squares, and serve.

Makes 12–16
Preparation 30 min
+ 2 hr to set
Cooking 25–30 min
Level 2

This is a chocolate variation on the classic panforte which originally comes from the beautiful Italian city of Siena.

chocolate panforte

Cake

- 1½ cups (225 g) all-purpose (plain) flour
- ¼ cup (30 g) unsweetened cocoa powder
- 1 teaspoon baking powder
- 1 teaspoon baking soda (bicarbonate of soda)
- 1 teaspoon pumpkin pie spice or allspice
- 3 large eggs, lightly beaten
- 1 cup (200 g) firmly packed brown sugar
- ½ cup (120 ml) sour cream
- ⅓ cup (90 ml) vegetable oil
- 1 teaspoon vanilla extract (essence)
- 2 cups (300 g) coarsely grated beets (beetroot/red beet)

Chocolate Glaze

- 5 ounces (150 g) dark chocolate, coarsely chopped
- ⅓ cup (90 ml) light (single) cream
- ½ teaspoon vanilla extract (essence)

Cake: Preheat the oven to 325°F (170°C/gas 3). Lightly grease a 9-inch (23-cm) springform pan. Line the base with parchment paper.

Sift the flour, cocoa, baking powder, baking soda, and pumpkin pie spice into a bowl.

Beat the eggs, brown sugar, sour cream, oil, and vanilla in a large bowl with an electric mixer on medium speed until smooth. With the mixer on low speed, gradually beat in the flour mixture. Stir the beets in by hand.

Spoon the batter into the prepared pan, smoothing the top.

Bake for 1 hour, until a toothpick inserted into the center comes out clean. Let cool in the pan for 20 minutes, then turn out onto a wire rack and let cool completely.

Chocolate Glaze: Melt the chocolate, cream, and vanilla in a double boiler over barely simmering water, stirring occasionally until smooth. Remove from the heat and set aside to cool slightly.

Spread the glaze over the cake, allowing it to dribble down the sides. Slice and serve.

Serves 8-10
Preparation 30 min
+ 1-2 hr to chill
Cooking 1 hr
Level 1

For the best results with this cake, prepare it a day ahead and glaze just before serving. It becomes more moist and flavorsome if stored overnight.

chocolate beet cake

Cake

1¼ pounds (600 g) dark chocolate, coarsely chopped

1½ cups (375 g) salted butter, chopped

1 cup (250 ml) water

1 cup (200 g) firmly packed dark brown sugar

2 cups (300 g) all-purpose (plain) flour

½ teaspoon baking powder

4 large eggs, lightly beaten

⅓ cup (90 ml) dry Marsala wine or sherry

Glaze

5 ounces (150 g) dark chocolate, coarsely chopped

½ cup (120 ml) heavy (double) cream

1 tablespoon unsalted butter

1 tablespoon liquid glucose

Cake: Preheat the oven to 325°F (170°C/gas 3). Grease a 9-inch (23-cm) springform pan. Line the base with parchment paper.

Combine the chocolate, butter, water, and brown sugar in a heavy-based pan over low heat. Stir until melted and the sugar has dissolved. Set aside to cool for 30 minutes.

Add the flour, baking powder, eggs, and Marsala, stirring until just combined. Spoon the batter into the prepared pan.

Bake for 45–55 minutes, until a toothpick inserted into the center comes out clean. Let the cake cool completely in the pan on a wire rack, about 1 hour.

Glaze: Combine the chocolate, cream, butter, and liquid glucose in a heavy-based saucepan over very low heat, stirring until melted. Let cool for 15 minutes.

Spoon the glaze over the cake. Let stand until set before serving, about 15 minutes.

Serves 12
Preparation 20 min
+ 2 hr to cool
Cooking 45–55 min
Level 1

This is a very rich cake. Serve in tiny slivers with small cups of strong black coffee. If liked, garnish with a few fresh berries.

chocolate mud cake

Cake

- 1¾ cups (275 g) all-purpose (plain) flour
- ⅔ cup (100 g) unsweetened cocoa powder
- 1 teaspoon baking powder
- 1 teaspoon baking soda (bicarbonate of soda)
- 1¾ cups (350 g) firmly packed brown sugar
- ⅔ cup (150 g) salted butter, softened
- 1 teaspoon vanilla extract (essence)
- 3 large eggs
- 1 cup (250 ml) milk
- 2 tablespoons strong black coffee
- 1 tablespoon dark rum

Mocha Frosting

- 5 ounces (150 g) dark chocolate, chopped
- 1 cup (250 g) salted butter, softened
- 4 teaspoons instant coffee granules, dissolved in 1 tablespoon boiling water
- 1 teaspoon vanilla extract (essence)
- 2½ cups (375 g) confectioners' (icing) sugar
  Chocolate-coated coffee beans, to decorate

Cake: Preheat the oven to 350°F (180°C/gas 4). Grease a deep 9-inch (23-cm) springform pan. Line the base with parchment paper.

Sift the flour, cocoa, baking powder, and baking soda into a bowl. Beat the brown sugar, butter, and vanilla in a bowl until creamy. Add the eggs one at a time, beating until just combined after each addition.

Combine the milk, coffee, and rum in a small bowl. Gradually beat the flour mixture into the batter, alternating with the milk mixture. Spoon the batter into the prepared pan.

Bake for 40–45 minutes, until a toothpick inserted into the center comes out clean. Leave to cool in the pan for 10 minutes. Turn out onto a wire rack and let cool completely.

Mocha Frosting: Melt the chocolate in a double boiler over simmering water, or in the microwave. Let cool.

Beat the butter in a bowl until pale. Beat in the coffee mixture, vanilla, and melted chocolate. Gradually beat in the confectioners' sugar until smooth and creamy.

Cut the cake in half horizontally. Spread the bottom half with one-third of the frosting. Place the remaining layer of cake on top and spread the top and sides with the remaining frosting. Make a decorative border with the chocolate-coated coffee beans. Slice and serve.

Serves 8–12
Preparation 30 min
Cooking 40–45 min
Level 1

This delicious coffee and chocolate flavored cake is perfect for special coffee mornings or afternoon teas.

frosted
mocha cake

Cake

- 5 ounces (150 g) dark chocolate, chopped
- 2/3 cup (150 g) salted butter, chopped
- 3/4 cup (150 g) firmly packed light brown sugar
- 1/2 cup (120 ml) cold water
- 2 large eggs, lightly beaten
- 1 2/3 cups (250 g) all-purpose (plain) flour
- 2 teaspoons baking powder
- 2 tablespoons unsweetened cocoa powder

Ganache

- 8 ounces (250 g) dark chocolate, chopped
- 2/3 cup (150 ml) heavy (double) cream
- 3 1/2 ounces (100 g) peppermint chocolate, finely chopped or grated

Cake: Preheat the oven to 325°F (170°C/gas 3). Grease an 8-inch (20-cm) round cake pan. Line with parchment paper.

Combine the chocolate, butter, sugar, and water in a saucepan over medium-low heat. Cook and stir until smooth, 3–4 minutes. Transfer to a bowl and let cool for 10 minutes.

Add the eggs to the bowl, stirring to combine. Add the flour, baking powder, and cocoa, stirring to combine. Spoon the batter into prepared pan.

Bake for about 50 minutes, until a skewer inserted in the center comes out clean. Let cool in the pan for 10 minutes, then turn out onto a wire rack and let cool completely.

Ganache: Combine the dark chocolate and cream in a saucepan over very low heat. Stir until smooth, 3–4 minutes.

Divide the mixture evenly between two bowls. Refrigerate one bowl for 2 hours, until firm. Leave the remaining bowl at room temperature for 2 hours, until thick enough to spread. Spread over the top and sides of the cake.

Roll heaped teaspoons of the chilled ganache into 12 round truffles. Roll in the peppermint chocolate. Arrange on top of the cake. Slice and serve.

Serves 10–12
Preparation 30 min
+ 2 hr to cool
Cooking 1 hr
Level 2

This cake has a subtle mint flavor from the mint chocolate used to decorate. For a stronger mint flavor, add 1 teaspoon of mint extract to the ganache.

mint chocolate
truffle cake

Cake

- 1⅓ cups (200 g) all-purpose (plain) flour
- 1 teaspoon baking powder
- 3 tablespoons unsweetened cocoa powder
- 1 teaspoon instant coffee powder
- ¾ cup (180 g) butter, softened
- 1 cup (200 g) superfine (caster) sugar
- 1 teaspoon baking powder
- 3 large eggs
- 2 tablespoons milk
- 3½ ounces (100 g) dark chocolate, melted

Frosting

- 1 pound (500 g) milk chocolate, coarsely chopped
- 2 cups (500 ml) heavy (double) cream

Decoration (optional)

- Coconut flakes
- Chocolate curls
- Unsweetened cocoa powder

Cake: Preheat the oven to 350°F (180°C/gas 4). Butter two 7-inch (18-cm) springform pans. Line with parchment paper.

Combine all the cake ingredients except the chocolate in a large bowl. Beat with an electric mixer on medium speed until creamy. Fold in the melted chocolate. Spoon the batter into the prepared pans.

Bake for 20–25 minutes, until firm to the touch. Cool in the pans for 5 minutes, then turn out onto a wire rack, peel off the paper, and let cool completely, about 1 hour.

Frosting: Put the chocolate into a bowl. Pour the cream into a pan and heat until simmering. Pour over the chocolate and stir until smooth. Let cool, then chill until thick and spreadable.

Split each cake in half horizontally to make four layers altogether. Sandwich the layers together with layers of the frosting, then spread the rest over the top and sides.

Decoration: If liked, sprinkle the top of the cake with coconut flakes, top with chocolate curls, and dust with cocoa powder. Slice and serve.

Serves 12
Preparation 20 min
+ 1 hr to cool
Cooking 20–25 min
Level 2

This rich chocolate cake is very easy to prepare. You can dress it up with coconut flakes and chocolate curls, or serve as is, depending on the occasion.

rich
chocolate
layer cake

Cake

- 5 ounces (150 g) good quality bittersweet dark chocolate, coarsely chopped
- 1 tablespoon espresso coffee
- ½ cup (120 g) unsalted butter, softened
- ½ cup (100 g) superfine (caster) sugar
- 4 large eggs, separated
- ¾ cup (120 g) all-purpose (plain) flour
- ⅓ cup (30 g) almond meal (ground almonds)
- Pinch of salt
- 1 cup (325 g) apricot preserves (jam)
- 1 tablespoon dark rum

Ganache

- 10 ounces (300 g) dark chocolate, coarsely chopped
- ½ cup (120 ml) light (single) cream
- 2 tablespoons unsalted butter
- 1½ ounces (50 g) milk chocolate, coarsely chopped

Cake: Preheat the oven to 325°F (170°C/gas 3). Lightly grease the base and sides of a 9-inch (23-cm) cake pan. Line with parchment paper.

Melt the chocolate and coffee in a double boiler over barely simmering water. Let cool for 10 minutes.

Beat the butter and sugar in a bowl with until pale and creamy. Add the egg yolks one at a time, beating until just combined after each addition. Beat in the chocolate. Add the flour and almond meal, stirring to combine.

Beat the egg whites and salt in a bowl until firm peaks form. Fold into the batter. Spoon into the prepared pan.

Bake for 40 minutes, until a toothpick inserted into the center comes out clean. Leave in the pan for 10 minutes, then turn out onto a rack and let cool completely. Slice in half horizontally.

Heat the preserves and rum in a saucepan over low heat. Strain through a fine mesh sieve. Spread half over the cut side of the base. Cover with the other half and brush the remaining preserves all over. Let stand until set, about 1 hour.

Ganache: Melt the dark chocolate, cream, and butter in a double boiler over barely simmering water. Set aside for 15 minutes. Spread evenly over the top and sides of the cake. Let stand until set, 2–3 hours.

Melt the milk chocolate. Use it to pipe SACHER on top of the cake.

Serves 8-10
Preparation 30 min
+ 3-4 hr to set
Cooking 40 min
Level 3

This famous Austrian chocolate cake was invented in Vienna by the master chef Franz Sacher for Prince Metternich in 1832.

sachertorte

- 1 (1½-pound/750-g) jar Morello cherries, in syrup
- ¾ cup (150 g) superfine (caster) sugar
- ⅓ cup (90 ml) Kirsch (cherry brandy)
- ¼ cup (60 g) unsalted butter
- 4 large eggs
- ⅔ cup (100 g) all-purpose (plain) flour
- ⅓ cup (50 g) unsweetened cocoa powder
- 2½ cups (625 ml) heavy (double) cream
- 2 tablespoons confectioners' (icing) sugar
- 1 teaspoon vanilla extract (essence)
- 4 ounces (120 g) good quality bittersweet dark chocolate, made into shavings using a vegetable peeler

Preheat the oven to 350°F (180°C/gas 4). Grease a 9-inch (23-cm) pan. Line with parchment paper.

Strain the cherries, catching the juice in a small pan. Add ¼ cup of the sugar and the Kirsch and stir over low heat for 5 minutes. Set aside ten cherries. Combine the remaining cherries and cherry syrup in a bowl. Melt the butter in a small pan. Keep warm.

Place the eggs and remaining ½ cup (100 g) of sugar in a double boiler over barely simmering water. Heat until lukewarm. Transfer to a bowl and whisk until very thick, 10–15 minutes. Sift the flour and cocoa into the egg mixture. Stir in the butter. Spoon into the pan.

Bake for 20–25 minutes, until firm. Leave in the pan for 10 minutes. Turn out onto a rack and let cool. Cover and chill for 4 hours, or overnight.

Slice the cake in half horizontally. Whip the cream, confectioners' sugar, and vanilla until thick. Drain the cherries, reserving the syrup. Combine 1 cup of whipped cream with the cherries.

Place a cake on a serving plate. Drizzle with one-third of the syrup. Spread with the cherry cream. Drizzle a third of syrup over the remaining cake. Set on the cherry cream layer, syrup-side down. Drizzle with the remaining syrup.

Spoon 1 cup of cream into a piping bag with a star nozzle. Spread the remaining cream over the cake. Pipe 10 rosettes around the cake and top with cherries. Sprinkle with chocolate shavings. Chill until ready to serve.

Serves 10
Preparation 1 hr
+ 6–24 hr to chill
Cooking 20–25 min
Level 3

Brimming with cream, chocolate, cherries, and Kirsch, this classic German cake is perfect for all sorts of special occasions.

black forest cake

Yule Log

- ⅔ cup (100 g) all-purpose (plain) flour
- ¼ cup (30 g) unsweetened cocoa powder
- 1 teaspoon baking powder
- 5 large eggs, separated
- ¾ cup (150 g) firmly packed light brown sugar
- 2 tablespoons water
  Superfine (caster) sugar, to sprinkle

Filling & Frosting

- 1 cup (250 ml) heavy (double) cream
- 15 ounces (450 g) dark chocolate, chopped
  Holly decorations

Yule Log: Preheat the oven to 350°F (180°C/gas 4). Butter a 10 x 15-inch (25 x 35-cm) jelly-roll pan. Line with parchment paper.

Sift the flour, cocoa, and baking powder into a bowl. Beat the egg yolks, brown sugar, and water in a bowl until thick and creamy. Fold in the flour mixture.

Beat the egg whites in a bowl until stiff. Fold into the batter. Spoon the batter into the pan. Bake for 10–12 minutes, until springy to the touch.

Put a large sheet of parchment on a work surface and sprinkle with superfine sugar. Turn the cake out onto the parchment and peel off the lining paper. Cover with a clean cloth. Let cool completely.

Trim the edges of the cake. Roll up from one of the long sides, rolling the paper inside the cake.

Filling & Frosting: Bring the cream to a boil in a small pan. Remove from the heat and add 14 ounces (400 g) of the chocolate, stirring until smooth. Let cool, then chill for 1 hour.

Grate the remaining chocolate. Spoon a third of the frosting into a bowl. Stir in the chocolate and spread over the unrolled cake. Roll up again. Set, seamside down, on a board.

Cut a thick diagonal slice off one end of the cake. Transfer the larger piece of cake to a serving plate. Spread frosting over the cut side of the small piece and fix it to the roll like a branch. Spread with frosting.

Serves 10-12
Preparation 30 min
+ 1 hr to chill
Cooking 10-12 min
Level 3

A yule log is a large piece of wood that is traditionally burned in the hearth at Christmas time. This cake is named for the log. Serve it on Christmas Eve.

chocolate
yule log

Cheesecake

- 1⅓ cups (200 g) graham cracker or digestive biscuit crumbs
- ⅓ cup (90 g) unsalted butter melted
- 14 ounces (400 g) white chocolate, coarsely chopped + extra, to decorate
- 1 cup (250 ml) heavy (double) cream
- 1½ cups (375 g) cream cheese, softened
- 4 large eggs
- 1 teaspoon vanilla extract (essence)
  White chocolate curls, to decorate

Raspberry Coulis

- 2 cups (300 g) fresh raspberries
- 2 tablespoons confectioners' (icing) sugar
- 2 tablespoons freshly squeezed lemon juice

Cheesecake: Preheat the oven to 350°F (180°C/gas 4). Line the base of a 9-inch (23-cm) springform pan with baking parchment.

Chop the cookie crumbs and butter in a food processor until they resemble bread crumbs. Transfer the mixture to the prepared pan and press down firmly. Bake for 10 minutes. Let cool.

Reduce the oven temperature to 275°F (140°C/gas 1). Wrap a double layer of aluminum foil around the outside of the pan.

Combine the chocolate and cream in a saucepan over low heat and stir until melted and smooth. Set aside to cool.

Beat the cream cheese, eggs, and vanilla with the chocolate.

Put the springform pan in a deep roasting pan. Pour the filling over the crust. Fill the roasting pan with enough boiling water to come halfway up the sides of the springform pan.

Bake for 1 hour, then turn the oven off. Leave to cool in the oven with the door slightly ajar for 2 hours.

Lift the cheesecake from the water, discarding the foil. Cover with plastic wrap (cling film) and chill for 4 hours.

Raspberry Coulis: Mash the raspberries in a bowl with the confectioners' sugar and lemon juice. Strain through a fine-mesh sieve. Decorate the cake with chocolate. Slice and serve, with the raspberry coulis to spoon over the top.

Serves 8–12
Preparation 30 min
+ 6 hr to cool & chill
Cooking 1 hr
Level 2

We have added a recipe for a delicious raspberry coulis to serve with this superb cheesecake.

white chocolate cheesecake

Strawberries

- 3 cups (450 g) strawberries, hulled, halved
- ¼ cup (60 ml) orange liqueur
- 2 tablespoons superfine (caster) sugar

Chocolate Roll

- 6 large eggs, separated
- ½ cup (100 g) superfine (caster) sugar
- ¼ cup (30 g) unsweetened cocoa powder
- 2 tablespoons all-purpose (plain) flour
- 3½ ounces (100 g) dark chocolate, melted, cooled
- 2 tablespoons milk

Filling

- 1¼ cups (300 ml) heavy (double) cream
- Unsweetened cocoa powder, to dust

Strawberries: Combine the strawberries, orange liqueur, and sugar in a bowl. Set aside for 3 hours to macerate.

Chocolate Roll: Preheat the oven to 350°F (180°C/gas 4). Brush a 10 x 12-inch (30 x 24-cm) jelly-roll pan with melted butter. Line the base with parchment paper, leaving 2 inches (5 cm) overhanging on the short sides.

Beat the egg yolks and sugar in a bowl until thick and pale. Sift in the cocoa and flour. Stir in the chocolate and milk until just combined.

Beat the egg whites in a bowl until soft peaks form. Fold into the chocolate mixture.

Spoon the batter into the prepared pan, smoothing the surface.

Bake for 10–12 minutes, until firm to the touch. Carefully turn out onto a sheet of parchment paper. Set aside for 5 minutes to cool.

Use a sharp knife to trim the edges. Starting from one short side, and using the paper as a guide, gently roll up the cake. Set aside for 5 minutes to cool. Gently unroll the cake.

Filling: Beat the cream in a bowl until firm peaks form. Spread over the cake and roll up. Dust with cocoa.

Slice and serve with the strawberries spooned over the top.

Serves 8
Preparation 30 min
+ 4 hr
Cooking 10-12 min
Level 2

This boozy roll makes a wonderful dessert for a grown-up dinner party.

chocolate roll **with** strawberries

Fondants

- 1 tablespoon hot water
- 2 teaspoons instant coffee powder
- 12 ounces (350 g) dark chocolate, coarsely chopped
- ¾ cup (180 g) salted butter
- ¼ cup (60 ml) hazelnut liqueur (Frangelico)
- 4 large eggs + 4 large egg yolks
- 1 cup (200 g) superfine (caster) sugar
- ½ cup (75 g) all-purpose (plain) flour
- ¼ teaspoon xanthan gum

Chocolate Sauce

- 3½ ounces (100 g) dark chocolate
- 1¼ cups (300 ml) light (single) cream
- ¼ cup (60 ml) hazelnut liqueur (Frangelico)

Fondants: Preheat the oven to 350°F (180°C/gas 4). Grease eight 1-cup (250-ml) dariole molds with butter. Place on a baking sheet.

Combine the water and coffee in a double boiler. Add the chocolate, butter, and liqueur and place over barely simmering water until melted and smooth. Set aside to cool a little.

Beat the eggs, egg yolks, and sugar in a large bowl with an electric mixer on medium-high speed until very thick and pale.

Gently fold the chocolate mixture into the egg mixture until just combined. Fold in the flour and xanthan gum. Divide the mixture evenly among the prepared molds.

Bake for about 15 minutes, until the surface is firm, but the puddings are still soft in the center. Remove from the oven and let sit for 5 minutes before turning out onto serving plates.

Chocolate Sauce: Combine the chocolate, cream, and hazelnut liqueur in a double boiler over barely simmering water, stirring until melted and smooth.

Spoon the chocolate sauce over the puddings, and serve immediately.

66

Serves 8
Preparation 20 min
Cooking 15 min
Level 2

These amazing little melt-in-the-middle chocolate desserts are so delicious you will make them time and again.

chocolate
fondants

Mascarpone Ice Cream

- 1½ cups (375 ml) water
- ¾ cup (150 g) superfine (caster) sugar
- 2 unwaxed lemons, zest finely grated and juice freshly squeezed
- 1⅔ cups (400 g) mascarpone

Chocolate Puddings

- 8 ounces (250 g) dark chocolate
- 1 cup (250 g) unsalted butter
- ¾ cup (150 g) superfine (caster) sugar
- 1 teaspoon ground star anise, seeds removed from pod, crushed in pestle and mortar
- 5 large eggs + 5 large egg yolks
- ⅓ cup (50 g) all-purpose (plain) flour
  Pinch of salt

Mascarpone Ice Cream: Combine the water, sugar, and lemon zest in a saucepan over medium heat and bring to a boil. Simmer until the sugar has dissolved then remove from the heat. Let cool a little then stir in the mascarpone and lemon juice.

Pour into an ice-cream machine and churn according to the manufacturers' instructions.

Chocolate Puddings: Melt the chocolate and butter in a double boiler over barely simmering water.

Beat the sugar, star anise, eggs, and egg yolks in a bowl with an electric mixer on medium-high speed until pale and creamy. With the mixer on low speed, gradually beat in the melted chocolate. Carefully fold in the flour and salt.

Pour the mixture into eight ¾-cup (180 ml) ramekins, filling each one half full. Chill in the refrigerator overnight.

Preheat the oven to 350°F (180°C/gas 4). Remove the puddings from the refrigerator and bring to room temperature.

Bake for 10 minutes, until the outside of the batter is set firm but the centers are still molten.

Serve the puddings hot with scoops of the mascarpone ice cream.

Serves 8
Preparation 30 min
+ 12 hr to chill
Cooking 10 min
Level 2

We have included a recipe for
mascarpone ice cream to serve
with these delicious little puddings.
But if you are pushed for time, you
could serve them with good quality
store-bought vanilla ice cream.

hot chocolate puddings

Pudding

- 1⅓ cups (240 g) dried dates, pitted and coarsely chopped
- 1¼ cups (300 ml) boiling water
- 1 teaspoon baking soda (bicarbonate of soda)
- ⅓ cup (90 g) salted butter, softened
- ¾ cup (150 g) firmly packed dark brown sugar
- 2 large eggs
- 1 teaspoon vanilla extract (essence)
- 1 cup (150 g) self-rising flour
- 2 tablespoons unsweetened cocoa powder
- 3½ ounces (100 g) dark chocolate, coarsely chopped

Chocolate Sauce

- ½ cup (100 g) firmly packed dark brown sugar
- 1 cup (250 ml) heavy (double) cream
- 3½ ounces (100 g) dark chocolate, chopped
- Fresh cream, to serve (optional)

Pudding: Preheat the oven to 350°F (180°C/gas 4). Lightly grease an 8-inch (20-cm) cake pan and line the base with parchment paper.

Place the dates, water, and baking soda in a medium bowl and let stand for 15 minutes.

Beat the butter and brown sugar in a medium bowl with an electric mixer on medium-high speed until creamy. Add the eggs one at a time, beating until just combined after each addition. Beat in the vanilla. With the mixer on low speed, gradually beat in the flour and cocoa.

Stir the date mixture and chocolate in by hand. Spoon the batter into the prepared pan, smoothing the top with the back of the spoon.

Bake for 40–45 minutes, until a toothpick inserted into the center comes out clean. Remove from the oven and let stand for 10 minutes.

Chocolate Sauce: Melt the brown sugar, cream, and chocolate in a small, heavy-based saucepan over very low heat, stirring until smooth.

Serve the pudding warm, with the chocolate sauce spooned over the top. Add a little fresh cream, if liked.

Serves 6–8
Preparation 20 min
+ 25 min to soak
Cooking 40–45 min
Level 1

Sticky chocolate date pudding
is a classic. Our recipe makes
a great family dessert for special
occasions. Serve with fresh cream
and berries to lighten it up a little.

sticky chocolate
date pudding

- 1½ cups (225 g) all-purpose (plain) flour
- 1½ teaspoons baking powder
- 3 tablespoons unsweetened cocoa powder + extra, to dust
- 1 cup (200 g) superfine (caster) sugar
- 1½ cups (375 ml) milk
- 1 teaspoon vanilla extract (essence)
- 1½ cups (375 ml) boiling water
- 2 teaspoons salted butter, softened
- Double (heavy) cream or vanilla ice cream, to serve

Preheat the oven to 350°F (180°C/gas 4). Lightly grease an 8-cup (2-liter) ovenproof bowl or pudding bowl.

Sift the flour, baking powder, and 2 tablespoons of cocoa into the prepared bowl. Stir in ½ cup (100 g) of sugar. Add the milk and vanilla and stir until well combined.

Combine the remaining ½ cup (100 g) of sugar and the remaining 1 tablespoon of cocoa in a small bowl. Sprinkle over the surface of the pudding.

Gently pour the boiling water over the back of a large metal spoon to cover the surface of pudding. Dot with butter.

Bake for 35–45 minutes, until a skewer inserted into the center comes out with just a few crumbs attached.

Dust with the extra cocoa and serve warm with the cream or ice-cream.

Serves 8
Preparation 30 min
Cooking 35–45 min
Level 1

This easy-to-prepare pudding is
brownie-like in flavor and texture.
Serve it warm with fresh cream or
vanilla ice cream.

chocolate
fudge pudding

Chocolate Crème Anglaise

- 4 large egg yolks
- 1 tablespoon superfine (caster) sugar
- 1½ cups (375 ml) heavy (double) cream
- 1 teaspoon vanilla bean paste or extract (essence)
- 2 ounces (60 g) white chocolate, melted

Soufflés

- 2 ounces (60 g) dark chocolate
- 2 tablespoons unsweetened cocoa powder + extra, to dust ramekins
- 5 tablespoons (75 ml) cold water
- 4 large egg whites
- 2 tablespoons superfine (caster) sugar + extra, to dust ramekins

White chocolate Crème Anglaise:
Beat the egg yolks and sugar in a bowl until pale and thick.

Warm the cream and vanilla in a saucepan over low heat. Pour over the yolk mixture, beating all the time.

Clean the saucepan and pour the mixture back into it. Simmer over medium-low heat, stirring all the time, until thickened, 8–10 minutes.

Remove from the heat and continue beating for 1–2 minutes. Beat in the white chocolate. Pour into a bowl and cover with a piece of damp parchment paper to stop a skin from forming. Set aside.

Soufflés: Preheat the oven to 375°F (190°C/gas 5). Brush six ramekins with melted butter. Dust with extra sugar and cocoa. Chill until needed.

Melt the chocolate in a double boiler over barely simmering water, or in the microwave. Set aside.

Mix the cocoa and water in a small pan. Bring to a boil, beating constantly. Pour into a bowl and stir in the chocolate. Leave to cool.

Beat the egg whites in a bowl until soft peaks form. Add the sugar and beat until stiff glossy peaks form.

Fold the egg white mixture into the chocolate mixture.

Fill the ramekins with the mixture. Bake for 10–12 minutes. Serve hot, with the warm chocolate crème anglaise spooned over the top.

Serves 6
Preparation 35 min
Cooking 10–12 min
Level 3

We have included a recipe for
White chocolate crème anglaise to
serve with these eyecatching little
desserts.

chocolate
soufflés

- 5 large eggs, separated
- ¾ cup (150 g) sugar
- 2 cups (500 g) mascarpone cheese
- ¼ teaspoon salt
- About 30 ladyfingers (sponge fingers) (preferably Italian savoiardi)
- 1 cup (250 ml) strong black coffee, cooled
- 7 ounces (200 g) dark chocolate, grated
- Unsweetened cocoa powder, to dust

Whisk the egg yolks and sugar in a bowl until the sugar has dissolved and the mixture is pale and creamy. Carefully fold in the mascarpone.

Beat the egg whites with the salt in a separate bowl until stiff. Fold them into the egg yolk mixture.

Spread a thin layer of the cream over the bottom of eight serving glasses or bowls. Soak the ladyfingers briefly in the coffee and place a layer over the mixture on the bottom of the glasses. You may have to break the ladyfingers to fit in the glass or bowl. Try to make an even layer.

Cover with another layer of the egg and mascarpone cream and sprinkle with a little chocolate. Continue in this way until all the ingredients are in the glasses, finishing with a layer of cream and chocolate. Cover the glasses or bowls carefully and chill in the refrigerator for at least 4 hours, or overnight.

Dust with a thick coat of cocoa just before serving.

Serves 8
Preparation 20 min
+ 4-12 hr to chill
Level 1

This is the classic version of this much-loved Italian dessert. It contains raw eggs which can very rarely carry salmonella. To avoid any risk, either use pasteurized eggs or heat the yolks and whites to 160°F (70°C) in a double boiler for 15 seconds.

tiramisù

2½ cups (625 ml) heavy (double) cream
4 ounces (120 g) dark chocolate, finely chopped
6 large egg yolks
½ cup (100 g) superfine (caster) sugar

Preheat the oven to 300°F (150°C/gas 2). Combine the cream and chocolate in a medium heavy-based saucepan over low heat and stir until the chocolate is melted. Set aside.

Whisk the egg yolks and ⅓ cup (70 g) of the sugar in a bowl until pale and creamy. Gradually stir in the hot cream mixture until combined.

Place six ⅔-cup (150-ml) ramekins in a baking dish. Pour the chocolate mixture into the ramekins. Pour enough boiling water into the baking dish to come halfway up the sides of the ramekins.

Bake for 45–50 minutes, until just set but still just slightly wobbly in the centers. Let cool to room temperature, then chill in the refrigerator for at least 4 hours.

Sprinkle the crème brûlées with the remaining sugar.

Caramelize using a chef's blowtorch, or preheat an overhead broiler (grill) on high heat and broil briefly until caramelized. Serve while the topping is warm.

Serves 6
Preparation 20 min
+ 4 hr to chill
Cooking 50–60 min
Level 2

Crème brûlée, which translates literally as "burnt cream," is a classic French dessert. This recipe is a dark chocolate variation on the traditional vanilla flavor.

chocolate
crème brûlée

Hokey Pokey

- 5 tablespoons sugar
- 2 tablespoons light corn (golden) syrup
- 1 teaspoon baking soda (bicarbonate of soda)

Mousse

- 8 ounces (250 g) dark chocolate
- 4 large eggs, separated
- 2/3 cup (150 ml) heavy (double) cream

Hokey Pokey: Oil a baking sheet. Heat the sugar and syrup gently in a heavy-based saucepan until the sugar melts, then simmer the mixture until it turns a deep, golden caramel.

Whisk in the baking soda (this will make it foam up), then quickly pour the mixture onto the prepared baking sheet, set on a wire rack, and let cool.

Mousse: Melt the chocolate in a double boiler over barely simmering water. Remove from the heat and stir in the egg yolks. Softly whip the cream and fold it into the chocolate mixture.

Beat the egg whites until stiff and fold them into the chocolate mixture.

Divide evenly among six to eight small serving glasses or cups. Cover and chill in the refrigerator for 4 hours.

Break the hokey pokey into small chunks and use it to garnish the tops of the mousses just before serving.

Serves 6–8
Preparation 30 min
+ 4 hr to chill
Cooking 5–10 min
Level 1

Hokey pokey is the New Zealand expression for honeycomb toffee. It is easy to make and children will love helping to prepare it because it bubbles up so spectacularly when you add the baking soda to the sugar mixture.

choco-mousse
with hokey pokey

Ice Cream

- ¼ cup (30 g) toasted (unsalted) hazelnuts + extra, to garnish
- 2 tablespoons confectioners' (icing) sugar
- 3½ ounces (100 g) dark chocolate, chopped
- 4 large egg yolks
- ¾ cup (150 g) sugar
- 2½ cups (600 ml) milk
- ½ cup (120 ml) heavy (double) cream

Chocolate Sauce

- 4 ounces (120 g) dark chocolate, grated
- ¾ cup (180 ml) milk
- 2 scant teaspoons cornstarch (cornflour)
- ¼ cup (50 g) superfine (caster) sugar

Ice Cream: Chop the hazelnuts and confectioners' sugar in a food processor until smooth.

Melt the chocolate in a double boiler over barely simmering water, or in the microwave. Stir into the hazelnut mixture and set aside.

Beat the egg yolks and sugar in a bowl with an electric mixer on high speed until pale and thick.

Place the milk and cream in a pan over medium heat and bring to a boil. Pour the hot milk mixture over the egg mixture, whisking constantly. Return to low heat and stir until it coats the back of a metal spoon. The mixture should not boil.

Pour a little of the hot milk mixture into the chocolate mixture. Stir well then pour the chocolate mixture into the hot milk. Whisk until cool. Chill in the refrigerator for 30 minutes.

Transfer to an ice cream machine and churn following the manufacturer's instructions.

Chocolate Sauce: Combine the chocolate and half the milk in a saucepan over medium heat and bring to a boil.

Dissolve the cornstarch in the remaining milk and mix into the chocolate along with the sugar. Stir over low heat until thickened. Remove from the heat and whisk until smooth.

Scoop the ice cream into serving bowls and drizzle with chocolate sauce. Garnish with nuts, and serve.

Serves 4-6
Preparation 30 min
+ time to chill
Cooking 8-10 min
Level 1

We've added a yummy chocolate
sauce to this dessert, but you can
also serve it without.

nutty chocolate
ice cream

Churros

- 1⅓ cups (200 g) all-purpose (plain) flour
- ¼ teaspoon salt
- 1¼ cups (300 ml) water
- ⅔ cup (150 g) unsalted butter
- 4 large eggs
- 4 cups (1 liter) vegetable oil, to deep-fry
- ½ cup (100 g) superfine (caster) sugar
- 2 teaspoons ground cinnamon

Chocolate Sauce

- 4 cups (1 liter) milk
- 8 ounces (250 g) dark chocolate, coarsely chopped

Churros: Sift the flour and salt into a medium bowl.

Put the water and butter in a medium saucepan over low heat and stir until the butter melts. Bring to a boil. Add the flour mixture and cook, stirring, until the mixture forms a ball and comes away from the side of the pan. Let cool for 5 minutes.

Add the eggs to the flour mixture one at a time, beating until well combined and the mixture is thick and glossy. Transfer to a pastry (piping) bag fitted with a ½-inch (1-cm) fluted nozzle.

Heat the oil in a deep-fryer or deep saucepan to 365°F (185°C). If you don't have a frying thermometer, test the oil by dropping a small piece of bread into the hot oil. If it immediately bubbles to the surface and begins to turn golden, the oil is ready.

Pipe 4-inch (10-cm) lengths into the hot oil and fry until golden. Remove from the oil with tongs or a slotted spoon and drain on paper towels. Continue until all the dough is cooked.

Combine the sugar and cinnamon on a large plate. Roll the warm churros in the cinnamon sugar to coat.

Chocolate Sauce: Bring the milk to a boil in a saucepan over medium heat. Remove from the heat and add the chocolate. Stir until melted and smooth. Divide the hot chocolate among serving bowls and serve hot with the churros for dipping.

Makes 24
Preparation 30 min
Cooking 15–20 min
Level 2

For a piquant touch, add ½ teaspoon of red pepper flakes to the chocolate sauce.

churros
with chocolate

2 (8-ounce/250-g) sheets ready-rolled puff pastry
8 tablespoons chocolate hazelnut spread (Nutella)
1 large egg, lightly beaten

Preheat the oven to 350°F (180°C/gas 4). Line a large baking sheet with parchment paper.

Cut each sheet of pastry into four squares. Spread 1 tablespoon of chocolate hazelnut spread over each square, leaving a ½-inch (1-cm) border all around the edges.

Brush the edges of the pastry lightly with egg. Roll up each square from corner to corner, pressing gently to seal. Stretch the ends of the pastry rolls a little to form halfmoon shapes. Place on the prepared baking sheet. Brush with egg.

Bake for 20–25 minutes, until the pastry is golden and puffed. Serve warm.

Makes 8
Preparation 15 min
Cooking 20–25 min
Level 1

Here's a quick way to prepare a delicious treat for a special breakfast or Sunday brunch.

easy
pain
au chocolat

- 1 tablespoon salted butter
- 3½ ounces (100 g) dark chocolate, chopped
- ½ cup (75 g) confectioners' (icing) sugar
- 1 (8-ounce/250-g) sheet ready-rolled puff pastry
- ⅓ cup (50 g) unsweetened cocoa powder, sifted

Preheat the oven to 400°F (200°C/gas 6). Line a baking sheet with parchment paper.

Melt the butter in a small saucepan over low heat. Add the chocolate and stir until smooth. Set aside to cool.

Dust a work surface with half the confectioners' sugar and place the pastry on top. Roll out into a 12 x 15-inch (30 x 38-cm) rectangle. Trim the pastry so that the edges are straight. Fold the pastry in half lengthways to mark the center and unfold it again, leaving a mark down the middle.

Pour the cooled chocolate mixture onto the pastry and, working quickly, spread it evenly over the top. Dust with the cocoa.

Begin to roll one side of the pastry rectangle into the center, to where the mark is. Repeat for the other side, until it meets the already rolled half. Dust with the remaining confectioners' sugar. Transfer to a plate, cover, and chill for 15 minutes.

When firm, cut the rolls into ¼-inch (5-mm) thick slices. Place on the prepared baking sheet, spacing them about 1 inch (2.5 cm) apart.

Bake for 8–10 minutes, until golden brown. Place on wire racks and let cool completely before serving.

Makes 12
Preparation 15 min
+ 15 min to chill
Cooking 8–10 min
Level 1

Palmiers, also known as palm trees or elephant ears, are typical of French, Italian, German, Portuguese, and Jewish cuisines, among others. This recipe adds a layer of creamy chocolate.

chocolate
palmiers

- ⅓ cup (70 g) superfine (caster) sugar
- 2 tablespoons unsweetened cocoa powder
- ¾ cup (90 g) pecans
- 2 ounces (60 g) dark chocolate, chopped
- ⅓ cup (90 g) cold unsalted butter, finely chopped
- 1 large egg
- 2 (8-ounce/250-g) sheets ready-rolled puff pastry
- 2 firm, ripe pears
- 2 teaspoons all-purpose (plain) flour
- 1 teaspoon vanilla bean paste
- 2 tablespoons confectioners' (icing) sugar
- Heavy (double) cream, to serve

Process ¼ cup (50 g) of the sugar with the cocoa and pecans in a food processor until finely ground. Add the chocolate, ¼ cup (60 g) of the butter and the egg, and process to a paste.

Preheat the oven to 450°F (230°C/gas 8). Line a baking sheet with parchment paper. Place the pastry on the baking sheet.

Using a 9-inch (23-cm) round cake pan as a guide, cut out a round. Place an 8-inch (20-cm) cake pan in the center of the round, and, using it as a guide, score an 8-inch (20-cm) round in the pastry to create a border.

Quarter the pears, then core and cut lengthwise into 1-inch (2.5-cm) slices.

Place the flour, remaining sugar, and pears in a bowl. Spoon in the vanilla bean paste, tossing to coat.

Spread the chocolate mixture over the pastry within the scored round. Place the pear over the chocolate mixture. Melt the remaining butter and brush over the pears.

Bake for 15 minutes, then reduce the oven temperature to 375°F (190°C/gas 5) and bake for 25 minutes more, until the pastry is golden brown and puffed. Set the tart aside on a wire rack for 10 minutes to cool.

Dust the pears with confectioners' sugar, then, using a chef's blowtorch or under a broiler (grill), caramelize the sugar on the pears.

Serve the tart warm or at room temperature with the cream.

Serves 6
Preparation 30 min
+ 10 min to cool
Cooking 40 min
Level 2

Chocolate and pear go very well
together, as this delicious dessert
will show.

chocolate
tart **with**
pears

Base

8 ounces (250 g) plain chocolate cookies
½ cup (120 g) unsalted butter, melted

Filling

7 ounces (200 g) milk chocolate, chopped
½ cup (90 ml) heavy (double) cream
1 cup (250 g) chocolate hazelnut spread (Nutella), softened

Topping

5 large egg whites
1¼ cups (250 g) superfine (caster) sugar

Base: Lightly grease a 9-inch (23-cm) fluted pie pan with a removeable bottom.

Process the cookies in a food processor until finely chopped. Add the butter and process to combine.

Press the mixture into the base and up the sides of the prepared pan. Place on a baking sheet. Chill for 15 minutes.

Filling: Melt the chocolate and cream in a double boiler over barely simmering water, stirring until melted and smooth. Set aside to cool.

Spread the cookie crust with the chocolate hazelnut spread. Pour the chocolate mixture over the top. Cover and chill for 2 hours, until firm.

Topping: Preheat the overhead broiler (grill) in the oven on high. Beat the egg whites and sugar on medium speed until stiff and glossy.

Spoon the meringue over the chocolate pie. Broil until the meringue is just touched with gold. Let cool for 15 minutes before serving.

Serves 8–10
Preparation 30 min
+ 2 hr to chill
Cooking 3–5 min
Level 1

This pie looks impressive and can be served even on formal occasions. It is surprisingly easy to prepare.

easy chocolate
meringue pie

Tartlet Pastry

- 1½ cups (225 g) all-purpose (plain) flour
- ⅛ teaspoon salt
- ⅓ cup (50 g) confectioners' (icing) sugar
- ½ cup (120 g) cold unsalted butter, cut into small cubes
- 1 large egg yolk
- 2 tablespoons water, as required

Filling

- 8 ounces (250 g) dark chocolate, chopped
- 3 tablespoons heavy (double) cream
- 1 tablespoon almond liqueur or brandy (optional)
- 2 large eggs + 1 large egg yolk
- ¼ cup (50 g) superfine (caster) sugar
- 1 cup (150 g) coarsely chopped almonds

Tartlet Pastry: Mix the flour, salt, and confectioners' sugar in a bowl.

Cut in the butter or pulse the mixture in a food processor until it resembles fine bread crumbs. Add the egg yolk and knead or pulse briefly until the ingredients come together. Add the water and knead or pulse to obtain a smooth dough.

Press into a log, wrap in plastic wrap (cling film) and chill for 30 minutes.

Roll out the pastry on a floured work surface to ⅛ inch (3 mm) thick. Line six 4-inch (10-cm) tartlet pans with the pastry. Chill for 30 minutes.

Preheat the oven to 375°F (190°C/gas 5) and put in a baking sheet.

Line the crusts with parchment paper and pie weights and bake for 15 minutes. Remove the weights and paper and bake for 3–5 minutes more, until golden.

Filling: Melt the chocolate, cream, and liqueur, if using, in a double boiler over barely simmering water.

Beat the eggs, egg yolk, and sugar until light and frothy. Beat in the chocolate and fold in most of the chopped almonds.

Spoon the chocolate mixture into the crusts and sprinkle with the remaining nuts. Bake for 12–15 minutes, until puffed but still soft in the center.

Transfer to a rack and let cool for 5 minutes. Serve warm.

Makes 6
Preparation 45 min
+ 1 hr to chill
Cooking 30–40 min
Level 2

Serve these scrumptious little tarts
warm for dessert with a of dollop
of creamy yogurt, whipped cream,
or a scoop of vanilla or
chocolate ice cream.

chocolate
almond tartlets

index